The
Language
of
History

The Language of History

A Greenwich Village Artist Remembers 9/11

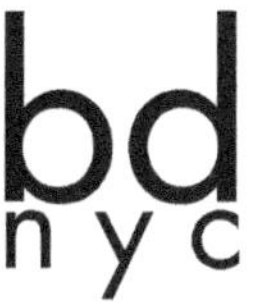

luke kurtis
introduction by Christopher Stout

Published on the occasion of luke kurtis's exhibition
The Language of History: A Greenwich Village Artist Remembers 9/11

at New York Public Library, Jefferson Market Library
425 Avenue of the Americas, New York, NY 10011
www.nypl.org

a luke kurtis/bd-studios.com production
Published by bd-studios.com in New York City, 2014
Copyright © 2014 by luke kurtis.

Introduction by Christopher Stout
Copy Edited by Karen Lea Siegel
Design by luke kurtis

ISBN 978-0-9890266-4-2

Table of Contents

Introduction

The exhibition accompanying this catalog, organized at The New York Public Library, Jefferson Market Library, has been designed to present artist luke kurtis's *Language Tiles* adjacent to the Library's permanent *Tiles for America* project.

While these two exhibitions with similar materiality may suggest themselves a metaphor for the original landmark World Trade Center Twin Towers, the *Language of History* catalog also contains the labyrinth of artistic thinking that has culminated in kurtis's *Language Tiles*: including documentary photographs, the artist's personal writings, video stills, poetry, and published media articles.

Not without dissention, the art world itself was one of the cultural "first responders" to the events of September

11th, as galleries in New York displayed formalized chromogenic prints canonizing the moments of impact and also images of the Twin Towers engulfed in flames.

In the creation of the *Language Tiles*, kurtis has investigated and reworked the striking original photographs taken by the artist just outside his apartment on 9th Street at 6th Avenue in Greenwich Village. kurtis is certainly looking for something additive to the traditional documentary narrative, and through this installation suggests a careful memorialization and honor to the living, and the dead, and also notably to the human process of grief.

Christopher Stout
Artist, New York
Founder of Bushwick Art Crit Group

The Language Tiles

The works on the following pages are inspired by the *Tiles for America* project that began at the corner of Greenwich and 7th Avenues near my home in New York City. As I began to put together the *Language of History* exhibition featuring my 9/11 inspired work, I felt the need to create new work for the show. But at first I thought, "What else do I have to say about the subject?" Not sure where to begin, on a whim I started to experiment with some collage techniques I had been developing for another as-yet-unexhibited body of work… and before long *The Language Tiles* were before me. Created using my original photography from 9/11 and printed as dye sublimations on ceramic tile, these pieces echo the *Tiles for America* in both topic and medium, yet reach beyond that tribute as well. *The Language Tiles* are my plea for a new hope—a new language—in our post-9/11 world.

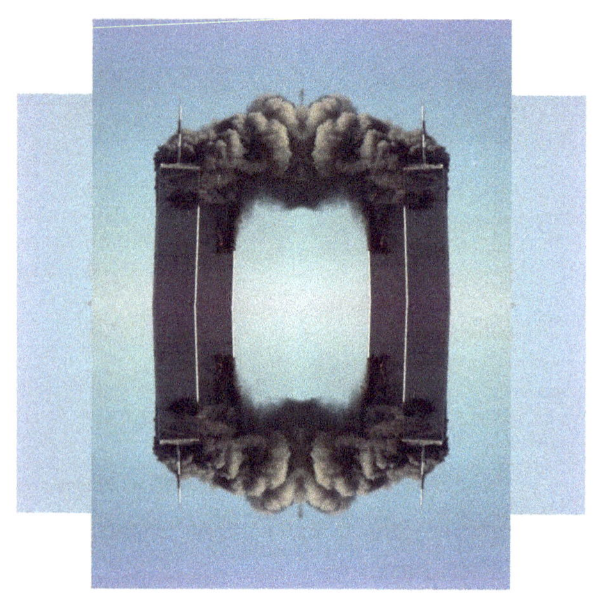

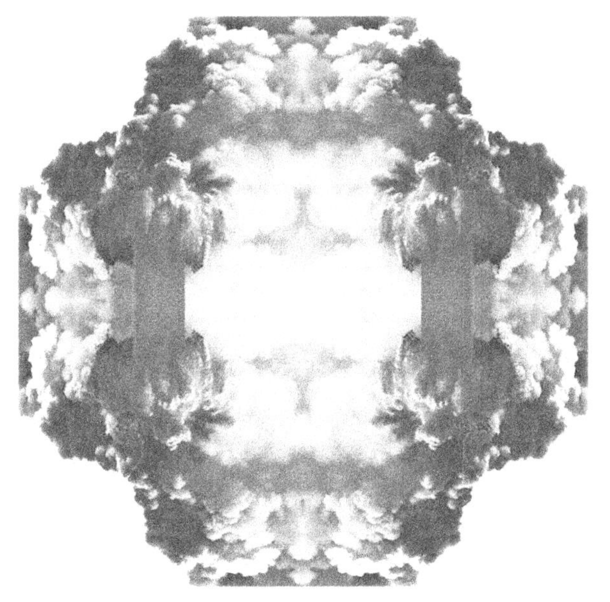

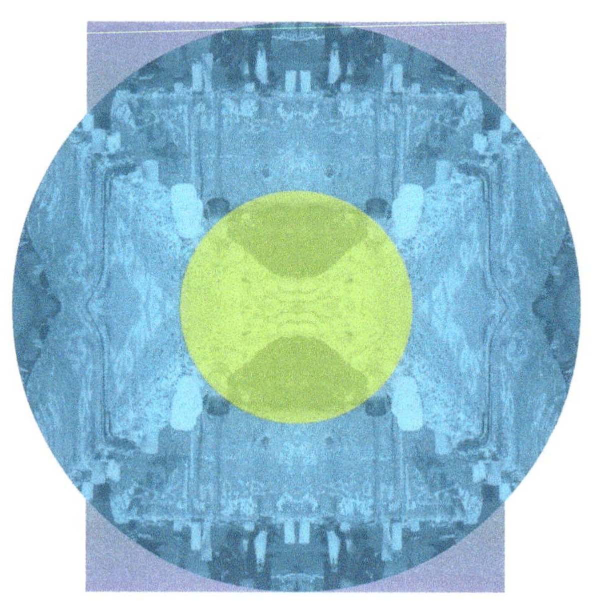

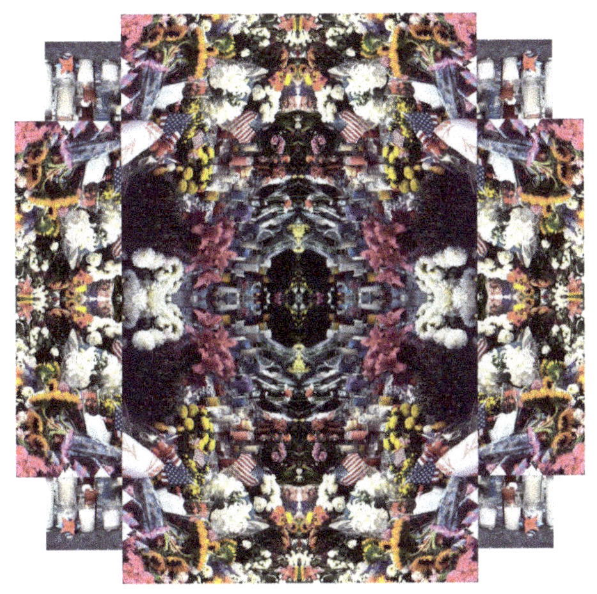

Photographs, Part 1:
11 Sep 2001

I created these photographs just outside my apartment on 9th Street at 6th Avenue in Greenwich Village. People were standing everywhere watching what was happening. Business as usual had halted with workers coming outside from their stores and restaurants. Throngs of people walked north, having vacated their jobs in Lower Manhattan. These photos haunt my memory. Yet their record of the events that day, as experienced from Greenwich Village, is important.

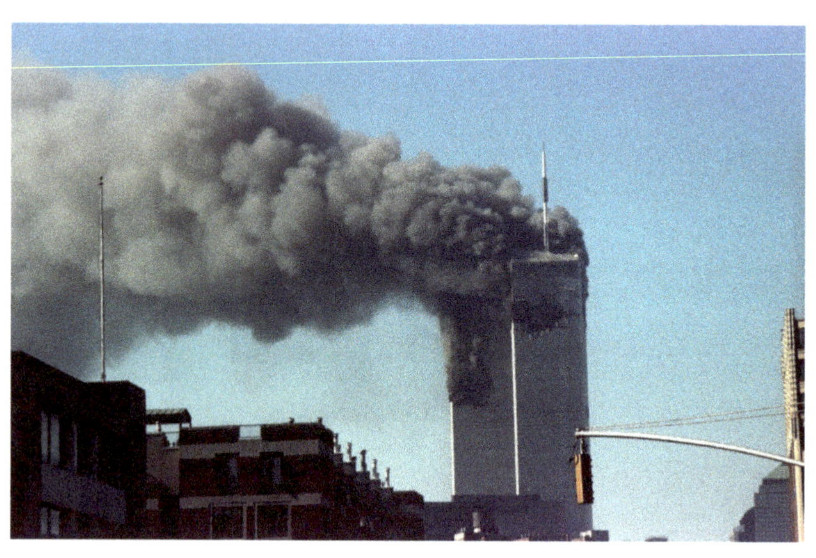

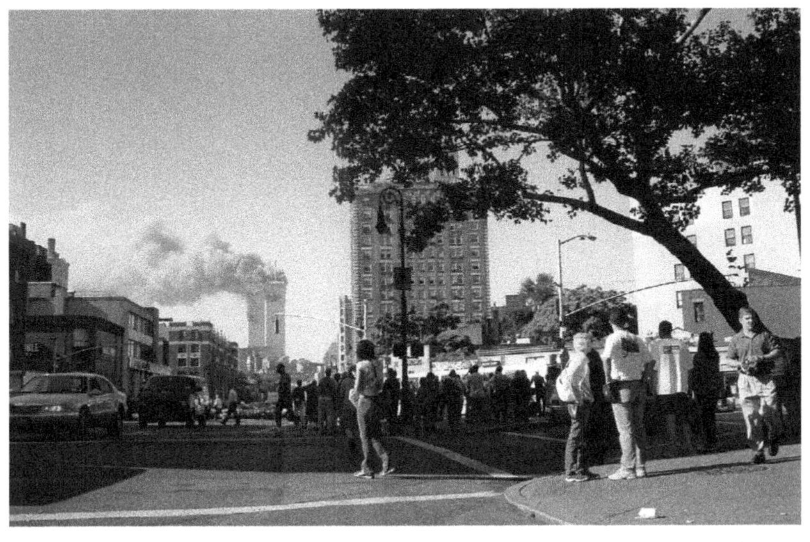

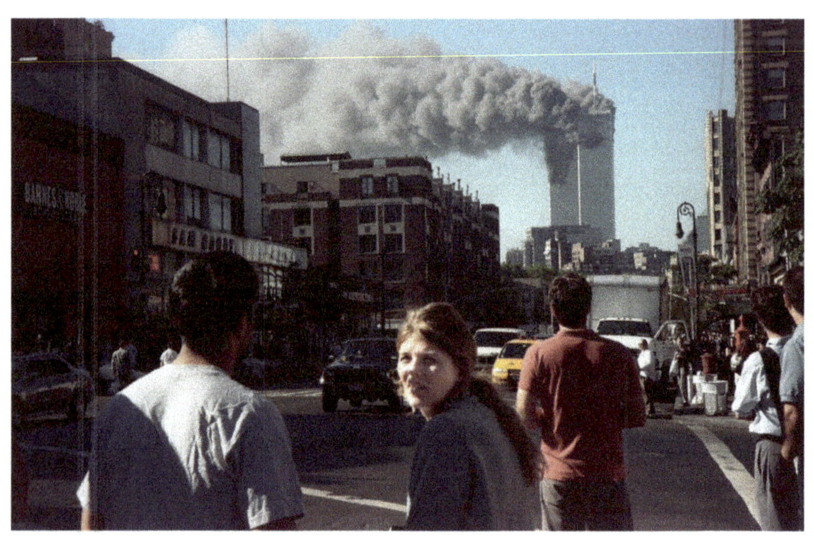

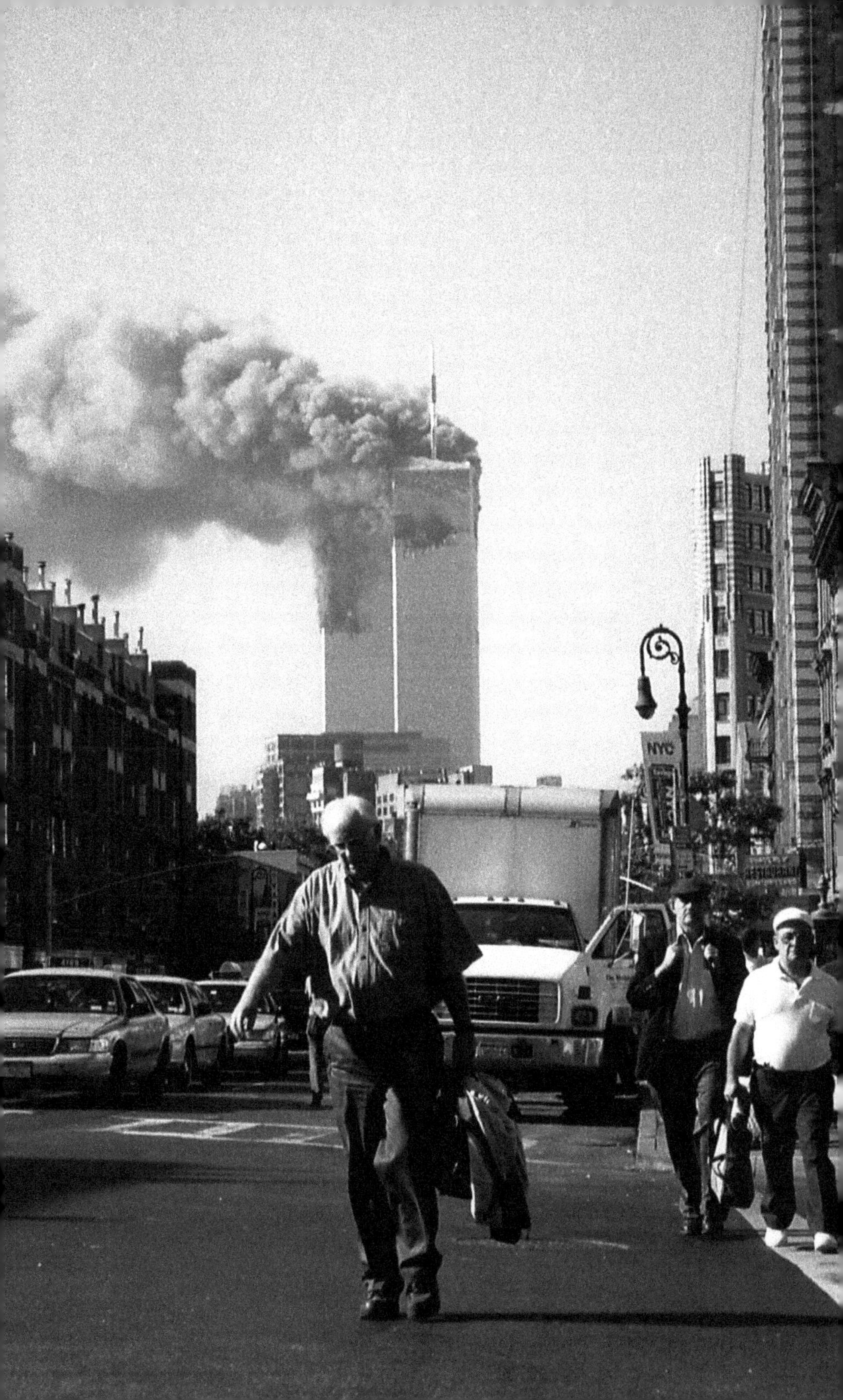

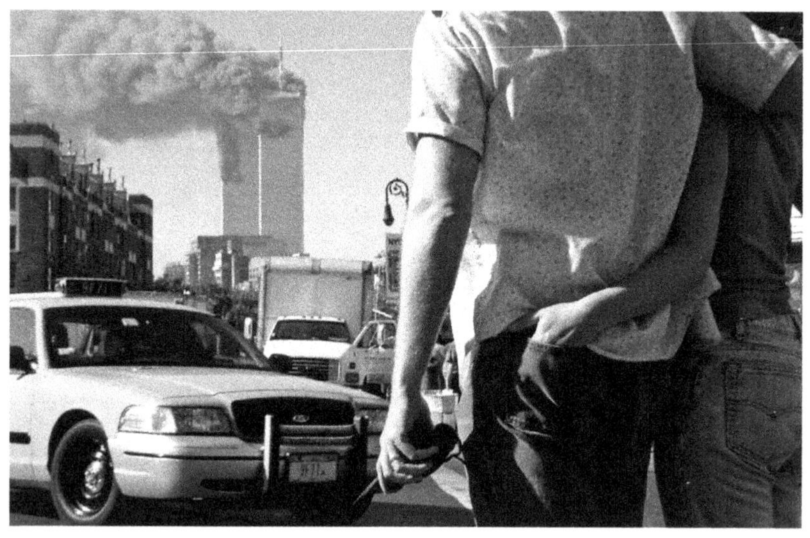

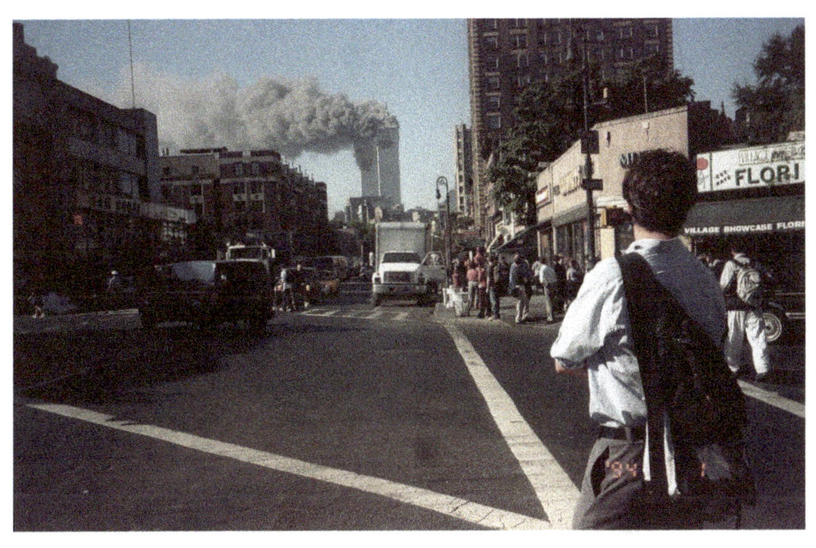

FLORI
VILLAGE SHOWCASE FLOR

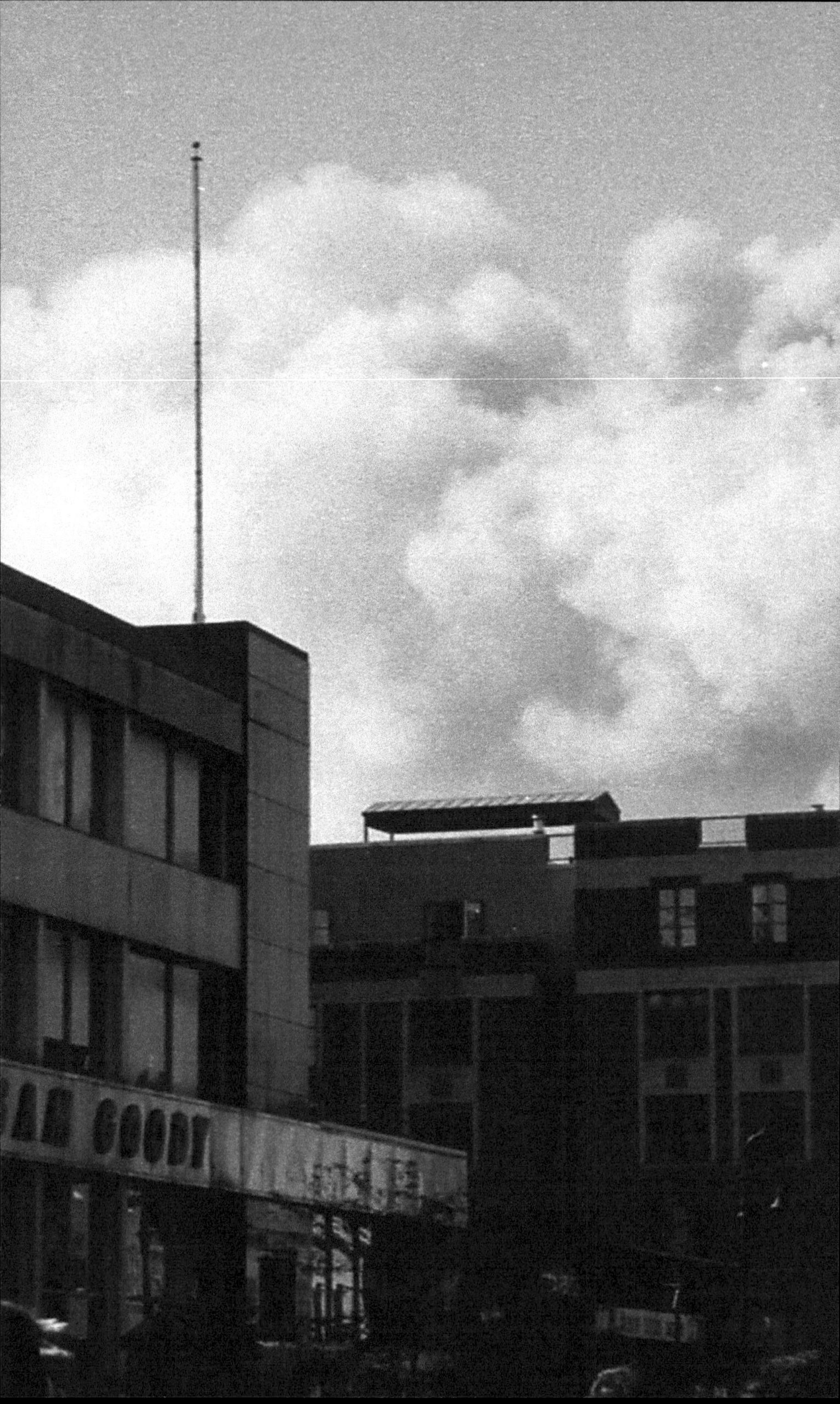

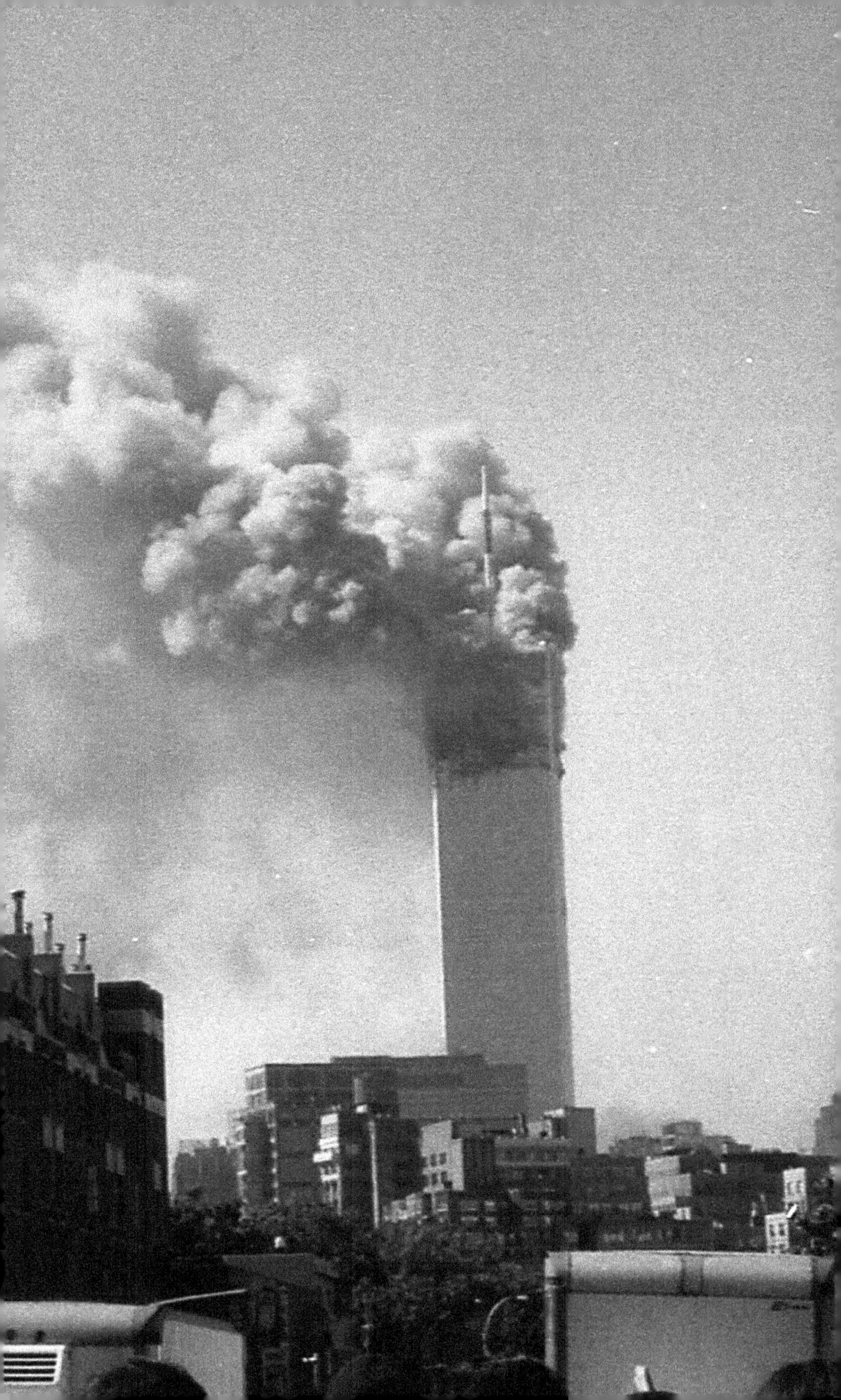

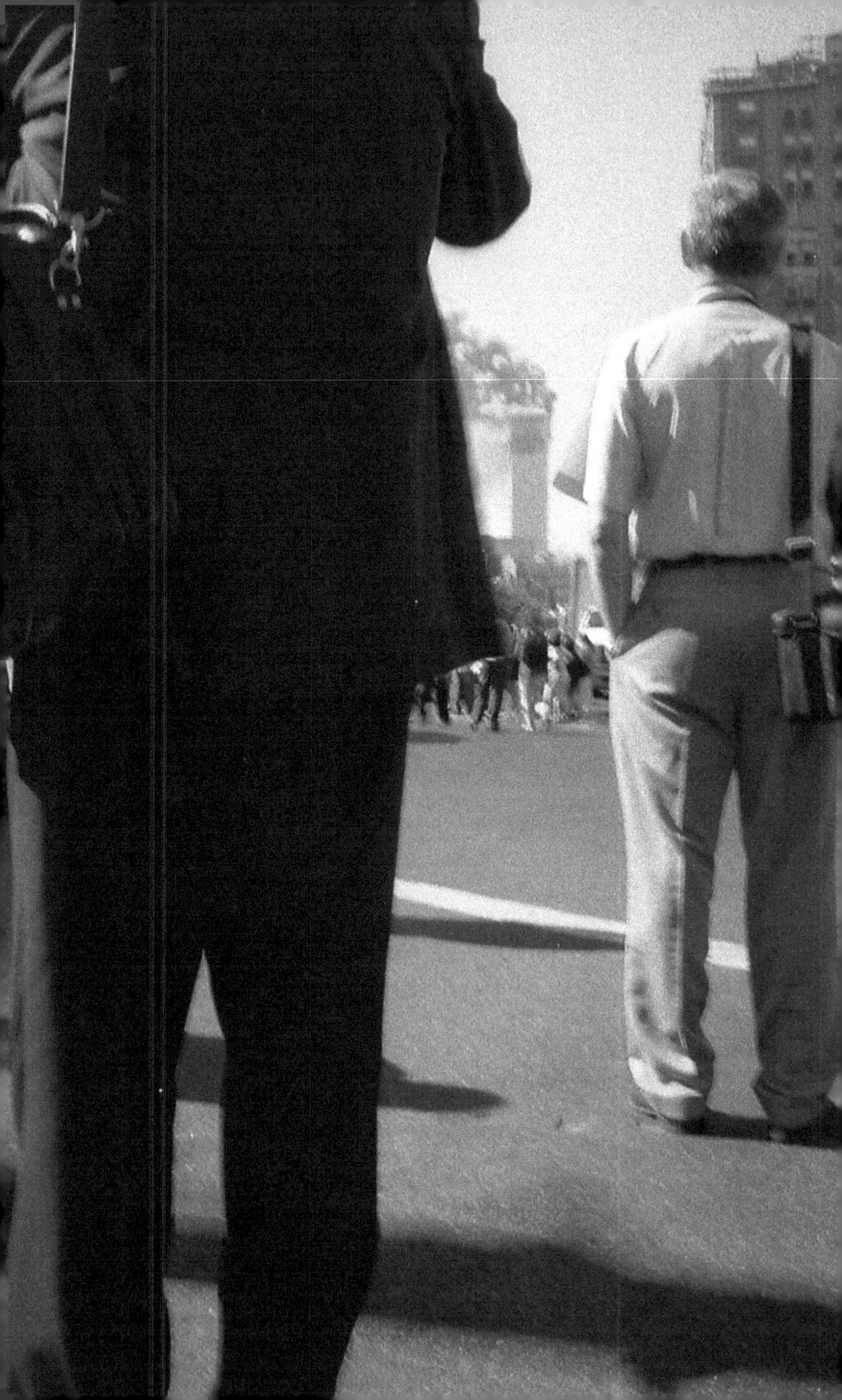

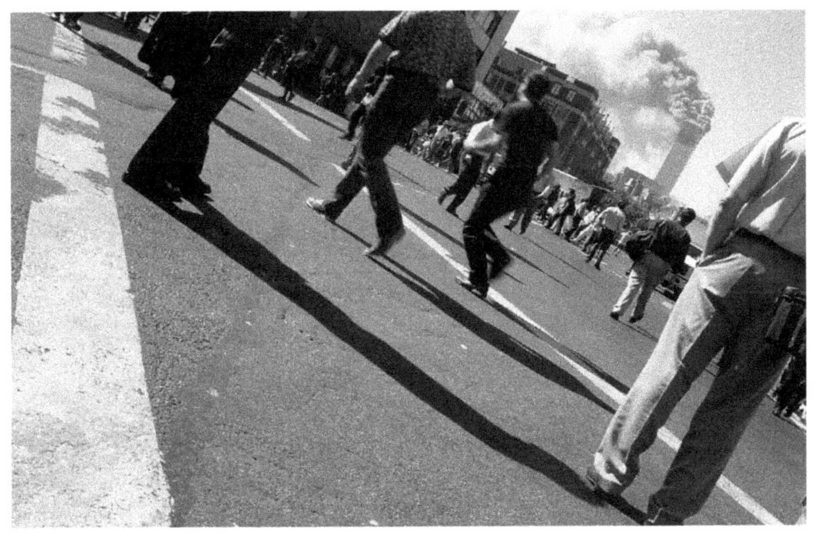

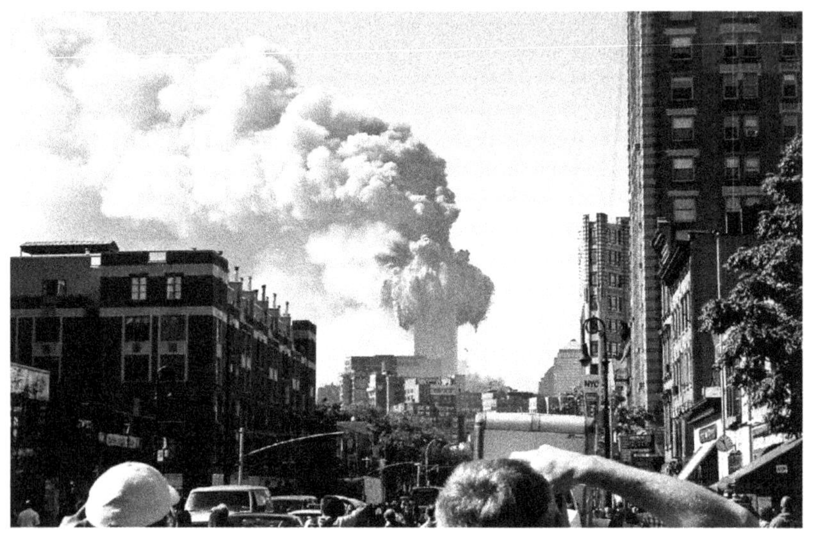

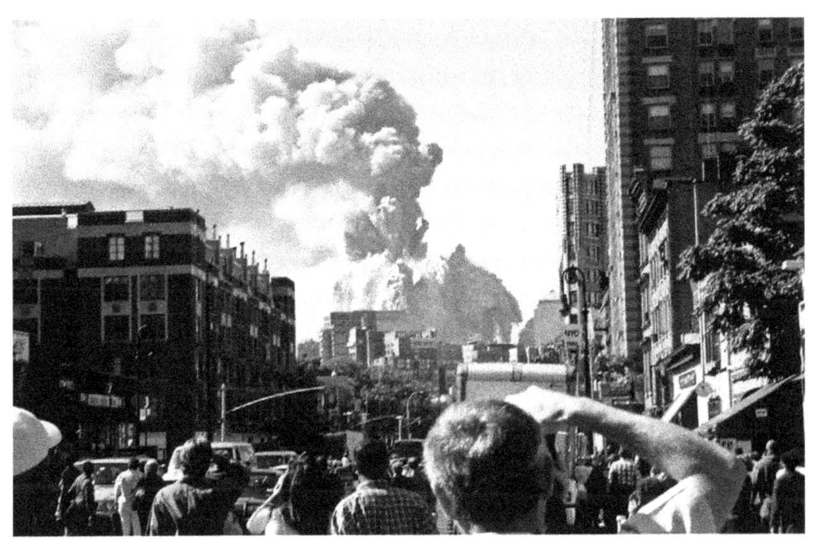

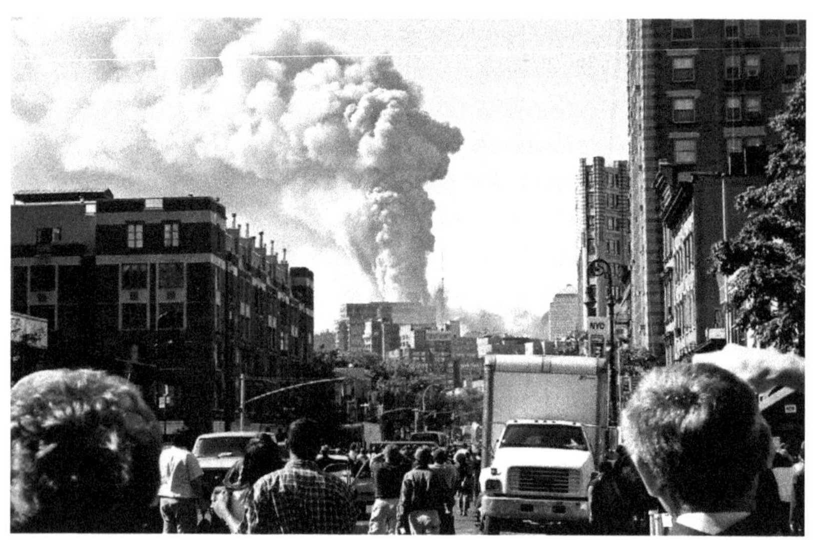

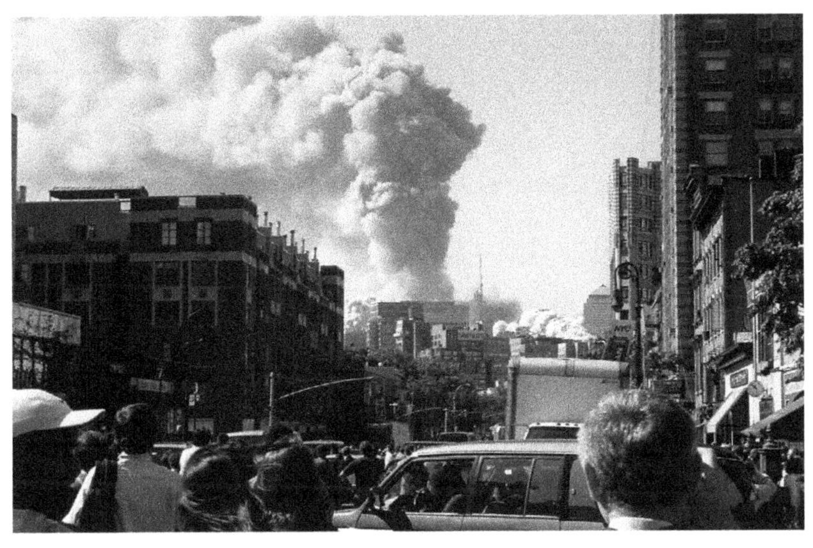

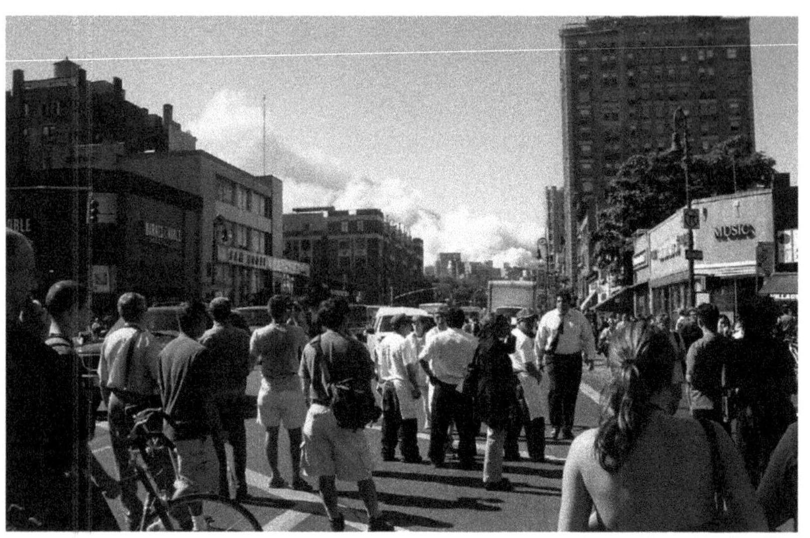

Media

The news media plays such a large part in how we perceive current events, history, and even the future. As soon as I saw what was happening on the TV the morning of 9/11, I popped a tape into the VCR and hit record. I let the tape run for the next six hours.

The stills on the following pages are from the tape I created that day and represent the way we were all glued to the TV waiting for word on what the hell was going on. This video also functions as an historical text. It's not just a document of *what* happened, but *how* it happened, the way it unraveled with all the drama and intrigue of a suspenseful movie. We were all in the dark. We didn't know what was happening… and that feeling isn't normally captured in traditional history books.

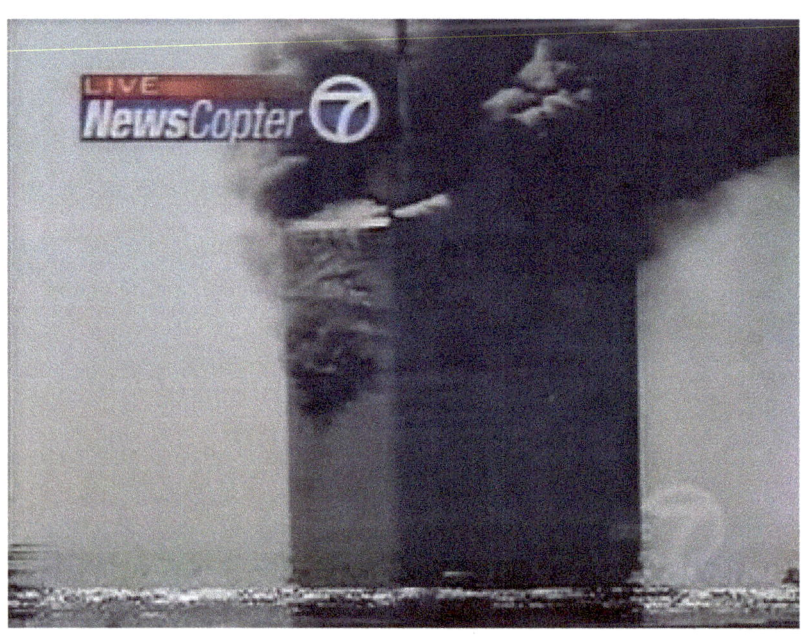
LIVE
NewsCopter 7

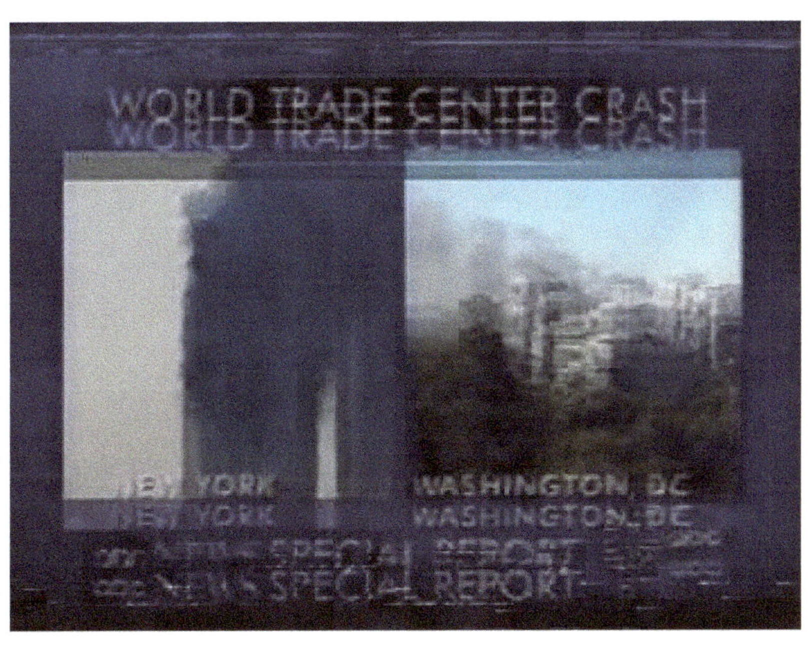

WORLD TRADE CENTER CRASH
NEW YORK
WASHINGTON, DC
NEWS SPECIAL REPORT

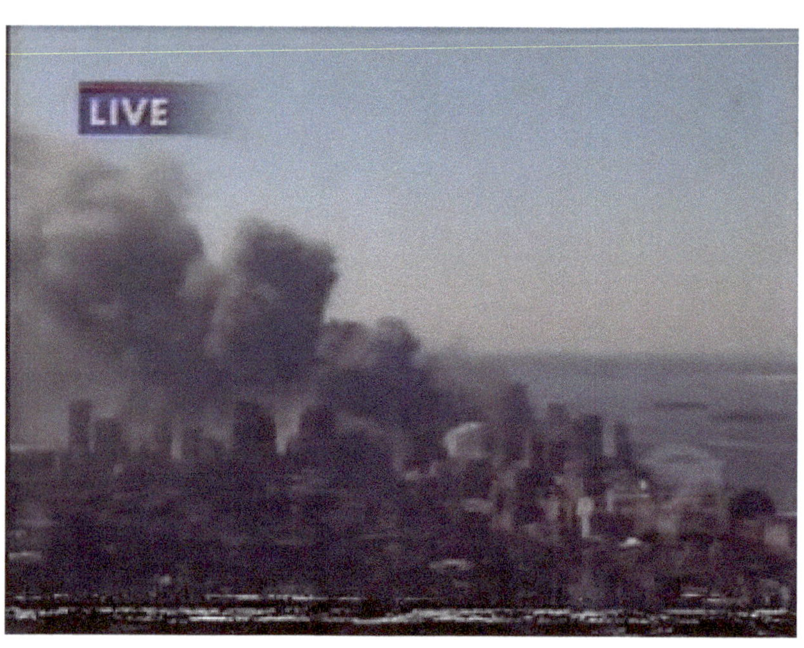
LIVE

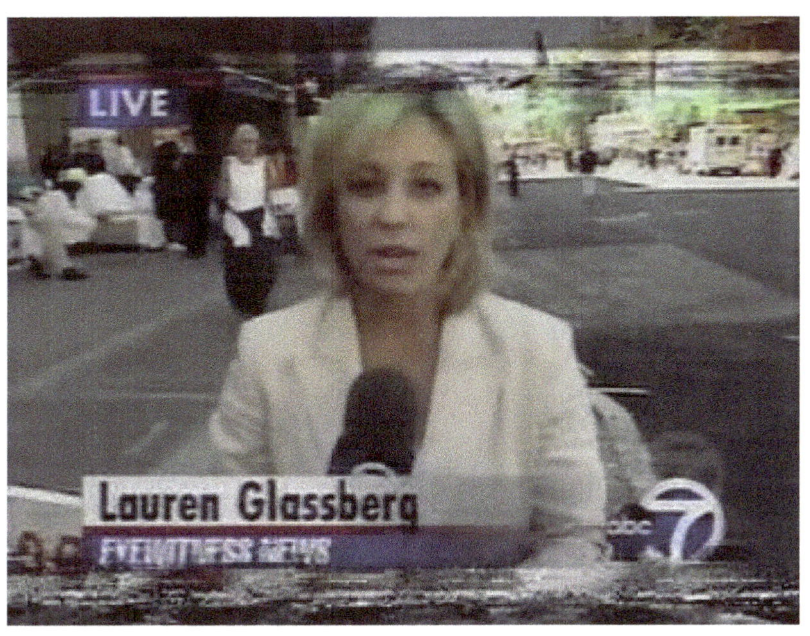

LIVE
Lauren Glassberg
EYEWITNESS NEWS
abc 7

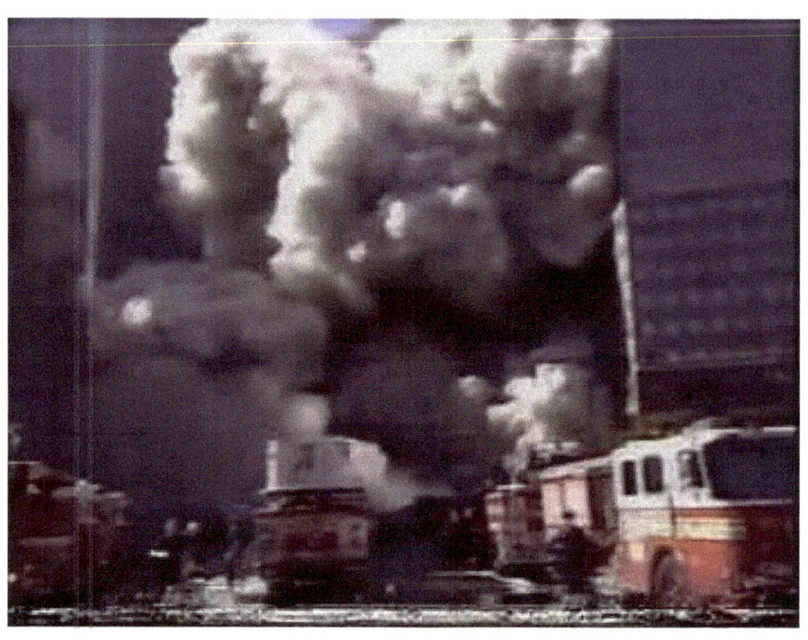

LIVE

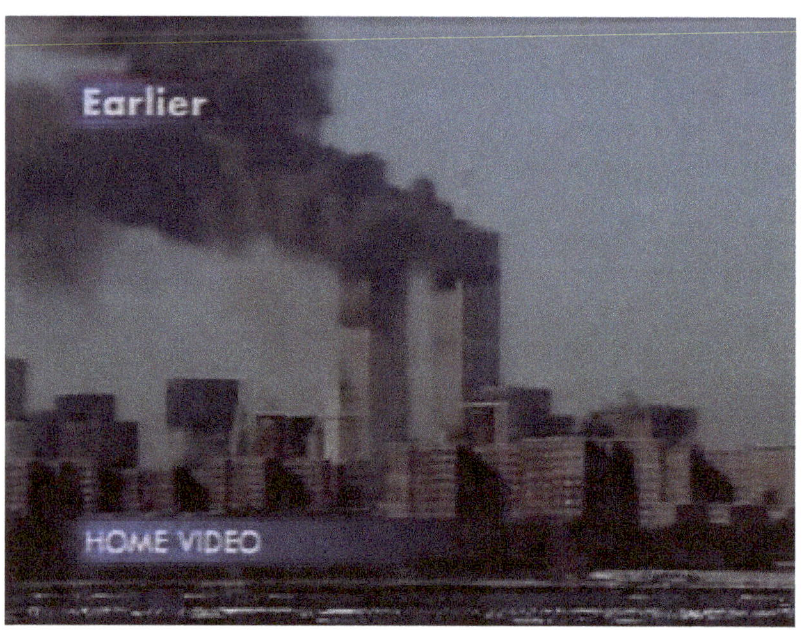

Earlier
HOME VIDEO

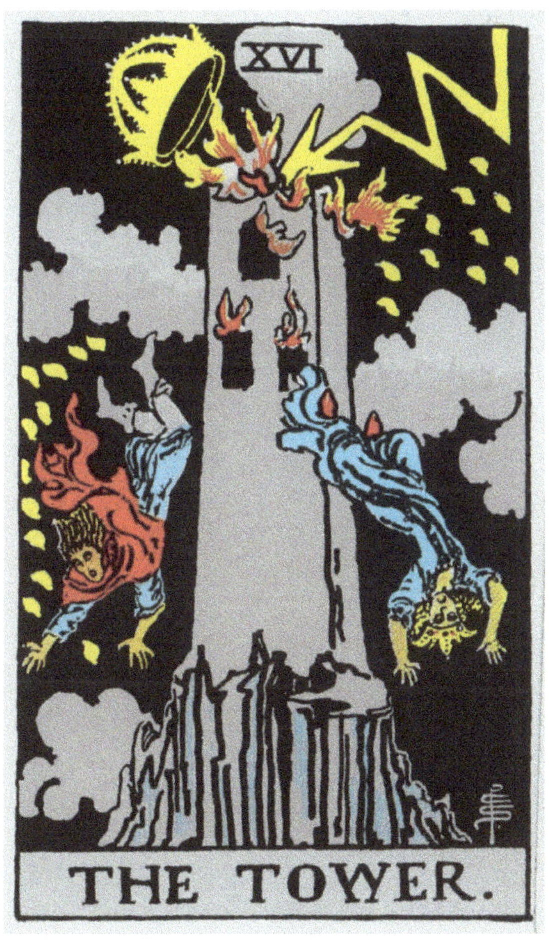

At one point that afternoon I pulled out my deck of tarot cards, shuffled them gypsy-style across the living room ottoman, and picked one card at random. I knew our world was in for great change when the sole card I drew was The Tower.

People back home, of course, were very concerned about me. L.D. Stafford of *The Chattanooga State Communicator* interviewed me about my experience (12 September 2001).

Words from NYC

By L.D. Stafford, Assistant Editor

Our copy editor, Faith Jones, is one of the many who have relatives in New York City. This office was fortunate enough to be able to speak with one of them. The following is an on-line interview with Jordan M. Scoggins of New York City. Mr. Scoggins lives at 9th Street and 6th Avenue in Greenwich Village. He saw the WTC collapse after being struck by two airplanes on Tuesday, September 11, 2001.

Q: What is the mood like in New York City?

A: "Streets are relatively empty except for people walking and moving very slowly. Very quiet. The whole scene of events feels extremely surreal. It does not feel real in any way."

Q: How much can you see from where you are?

A: "We live on the corner of 9th Street and 6th Avenue. From our corner you have a clear and direct view of the WTC, or where it used to be. I watched the second building crumble to the ground. It looked like a mushroom cloud falling towards the earth. I had my camera and captured it on film, too."

Q: Will New York City recover?

A: "NYC will recover. We will all recover. This is an event that has hurt many people. It will cause great change, but positive results must come from it. Hopefully, it will rouse people to understand the importance of peace, and will cause all of us to wish and hope and actively work for such. If we wish it, if we all desire it, it will happen. We have the power to change the world."

Mr. Scoggins, despite what must be a sense of shock and loss remained positive and hopeful throughout the interview. We, at the *Communicator*, would like to thank him for sharing his thoughts and feelings with us.

The mainstream media, too, was full of stories about what we were all going through. I clipped this ad from the 19 September *New York Times* both because I found it humorous and because it seemed a bit too true.

43

Many people were misunderstood in the wake of 9/11. Karlheinz Stockhausen was attacked for referring to the attacks as "the greatest work of art ever." Stockhausen did not intend the remarks to be pro-terrorist or to say that he supported the attacks. Quite the contrary. He was merely getting at the idea at how deeply the terrorist acts impacted almost every person—something even the greatest works of art cannot compete with. He immediately realized how his words made light of the situation in a way he did not intend and retracted his statements. He requested the media not report them but this request was not honored.

Others artists brought forth their feelings in more productive if no less divisive ways. Deborah Solomon's article in the 30 September *New York Times* stands out in particular for me. In "From the Rubble, Ideas for Rebirth," Solomon collected ideas for the World Trade Center site from various downtown New York artists, including Louise Bourgeois, Barbara Kruger, Richard Meier, and James Turrell.

Some artists were in favor of a park, others were in favor of new office buildings.

"It would be absolutely cruel to build a building on the site," said Shirin Neshat. "In order to remember the loss of lives, you need a certain amount of emptiness."

Yoko Ono posted a message of peace in Times Square, proclaiming, "Imagine all the people living life in peace." As a pioneer of advertising-as-art, such installations are not foreign in her oeuvre and this installation in particular echoed her 1969 *War Is Over!* collaboration with John Lennon.

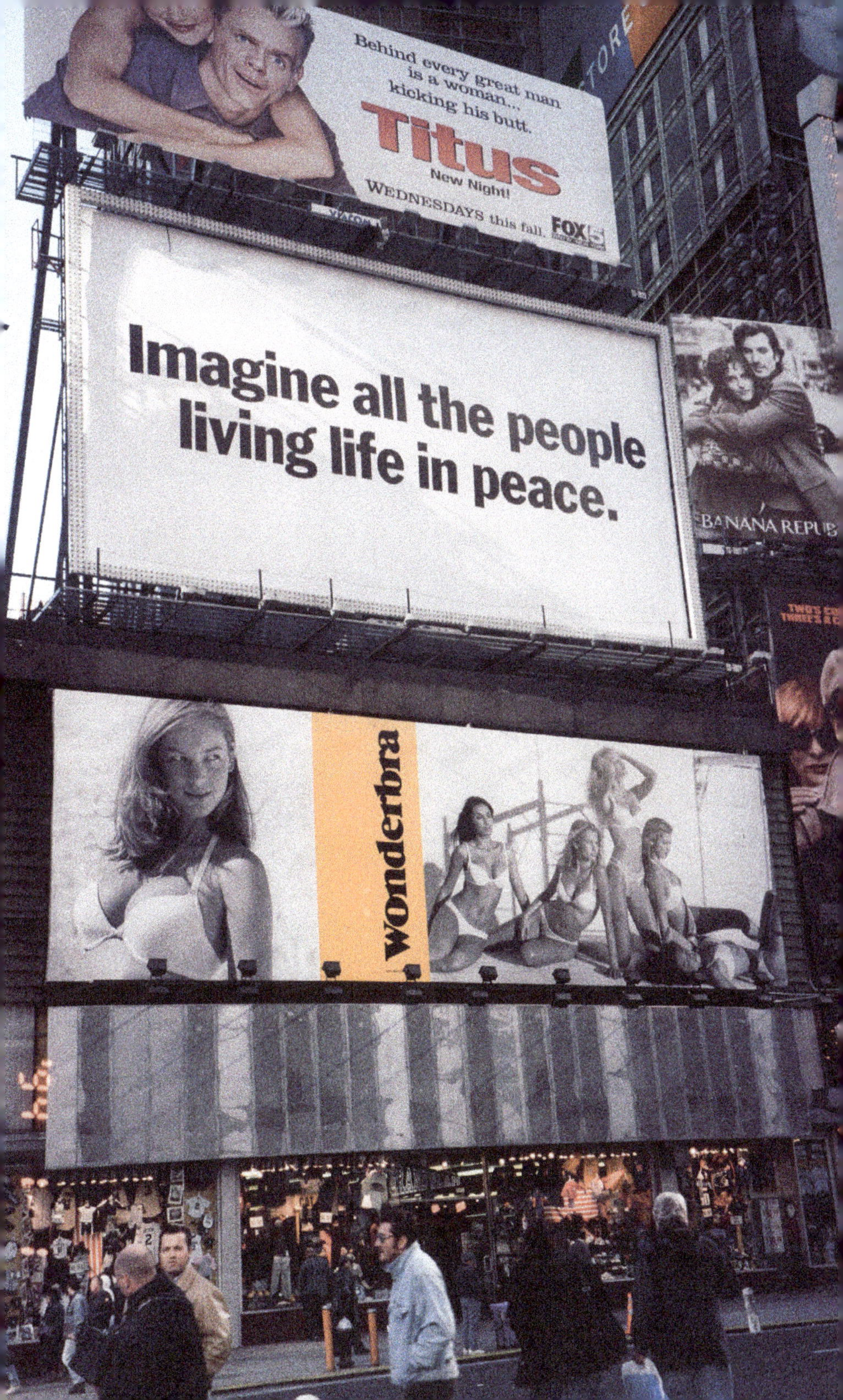

Behind every great man is a woman... kicking his butt.
Titus
New Night!
WEDNESDAYS this fall.
FOX 5
Imagine all the people
living life in peace.
BANANA REPUB
Wonderbra

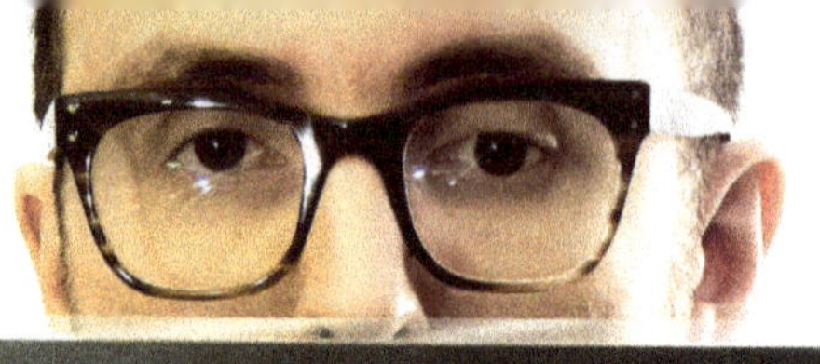

THE NEW YORK TIMES SUNDAY SEPTEMBER 23, 2001
A29
Imagine all the people living life in peace.

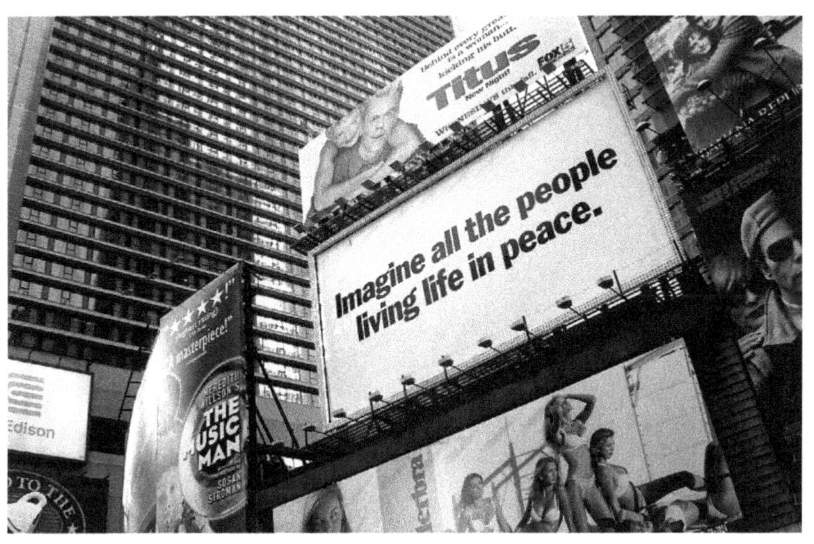

Ono also displayed the same work in a full page ad in the
New York Times on 23 September.

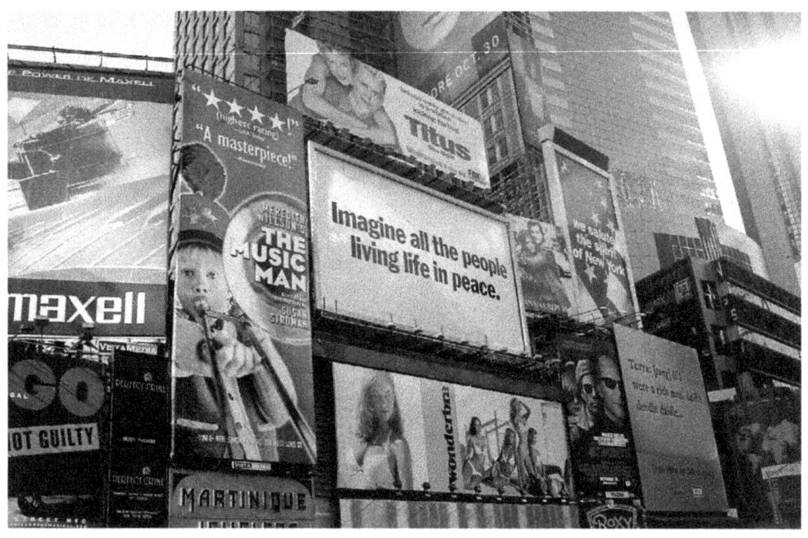
THE POWER OF MAXELL
maxell
GO
NOT GUILTY
A masterpiece!
THE MUSIC MAN
SUSAN STROMAN
MARTINIQUE
Titus
Imagine all the people
living life in peace.
the spirit
of New York
ROXY

Poetry

I was in shock. I thought, "If I'm ever to write again, I have to make myself do it now." And so I did. The words did not come easy, and even now words do not adequately describe what I felt that day and in the days after. But I knew I had to grasp for them. These poems are what happened when I did.

I composed "from only a mile away" only three days after the attacks. It's my poetic recollection of the experience. My "mile" is a metaphorical one (the corner of 6th Ave and 9th St is more accurately about 2.5 miles from the World Trade Center) and reflects how I felt no words were adequate to describe the way I felt.

from only a mile away

from only a mile away
i watched a tower fall.

i watched a dream
of cinematic scope,
worldly proportions
and fragile hope.

from only a mile away
i watched a tower fall

to rubble and disaster,
fire and flame,
bodies and hopes
and dreams deranged.

from only a mile away
i watched a tower fall

and now i see
a presence fly
to hope, to life
now towards the sky:

from only a mile away
i watched a pheonix rise.

I composed "as i sit waiting" after I arrived to class early one morning in the days after 9/11. This was the first time my class met after the attacks and uncertainty filled the air. The poem is less hopeful than the earlier "from only a mile away" and reflects a growing uneasiness about the future and perhaps reflects my first glimpse of the profound cultural transformation brought about by the catastrophic events.

as i sit waiting

there has been a—tragedy—here
and as i sit waiting—
         early to my day—
wondering if any among us—
         the living—
         are no longer with us.
there has been a—tragedy—here
which i watched from only a mile away—
         destruction; decay—
wondering how my life—
         the living—
         must—and can we?—move on.
there has been a—tragedy—here
now lost to a gothic tomb—
         early to death fallen—
and so are we now early?
         to victory?
         to rise?
there has been a—tragedy—
                              where?

I published *let us prey* in 2005. It collects a series of digital collage works and associated poetry ("bush", "autoatomicanxiety," and "cold congregation") that reflect my experiences and concerns in what had very clearly become the post-9/11 world. The texts from *let us prey* moved beyond the emotional reactions of the earlier "from only a mile away" and "as i sit waiting" poems and take on a decidedly more political tone. As a whole, the *let us prey* book captures the anxieties of the early post-9/11 years.

bush

our hussein,
who art in the east,
wretched be thy name.

your kingdom fell,
you would do well
to live than to die in vain.

give us this pleasure at your leisure
and forgive our intrusion.
you have our word; you have our trust.

lead us to your weapons,
for your land shall not bear
that which belongs to us.

amen.

autoatomicanxiety

the fear of bliss
is an immense
temptation

isolation is a struggle
against the odds of
extinction

where every distinction
between humans and lower
primates

between man and the apes
becomes blurred and
unclear

a disease of social disability
impolite civility and
death

every step every breath
an accomplishment a
triumph

immense and defiant
the world is plagued
diseased

loud detonation
from the mountains to the seas
everywhere

on land and on air
no place no one is
denied

the depths of disguise
the stoic dysfunction of
autoatomicanxiety

death and propriety
the slow release into
atmosphere

yes—it is here—
this deadly urge for
recompense

and the fear of this
is an immense
temptation

cold congregation

the need for atonement is immense
and your silent recompense
is inadequate

you've gone to battle with
all the freaks and whores
all the restless bores

you've marched against love
in the name of god
for a purpose you call religion

but tell me what's with this
your thoughtless abandon
of ceremony and grace

and how you show your face
is a mystery to me
the way you flaunt hatred

the question of god—of life—
i make no claim
but whether you do or you might

whether you love or you fight
there will be no peaceful amends
for such a cold congregation

Photographs, Part 2:
After 11 Sep 2001

In the days after 9/11, 14th Street—the border between the Village and Chelsea—marked the no-entry zone. You couldn't enter the Village without ID showing that you lived there. The next few pages contain some of my photos from the days after 9/11. While the areas immediately surrounding the WTC were certainly the most impacted, the experience reverberated throughout the city up to the Village and beyond as we all mourned the loss and began the process of rebuilding our identity as New Yorkers.

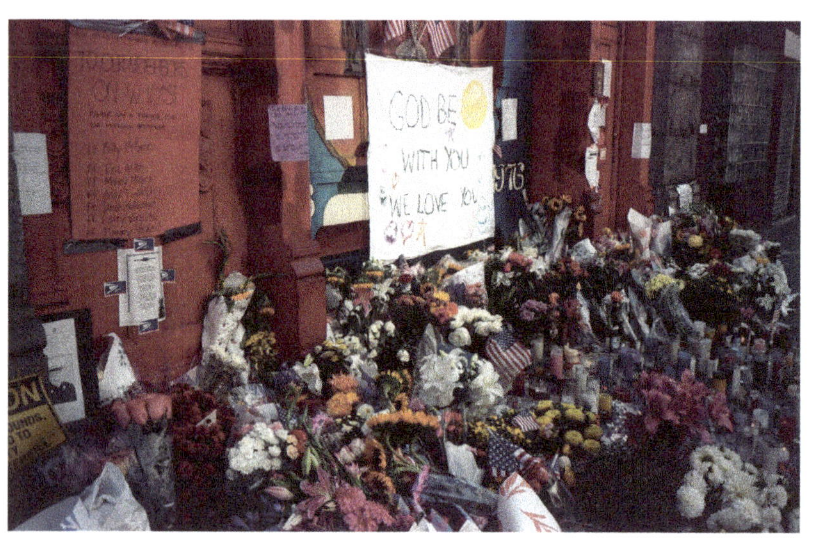

GOD BE
WITH YOU
WE LOVE YOU

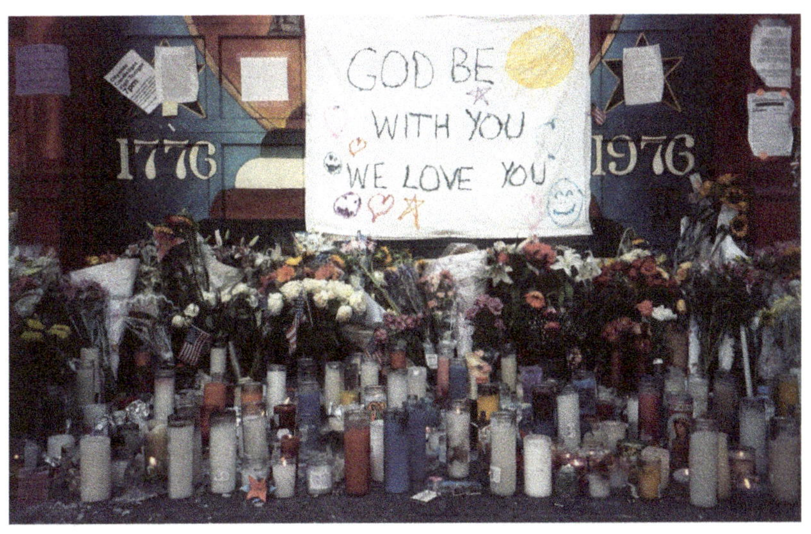

GOD BE
WITH YOU
WE LOVE YOU
1776
1976

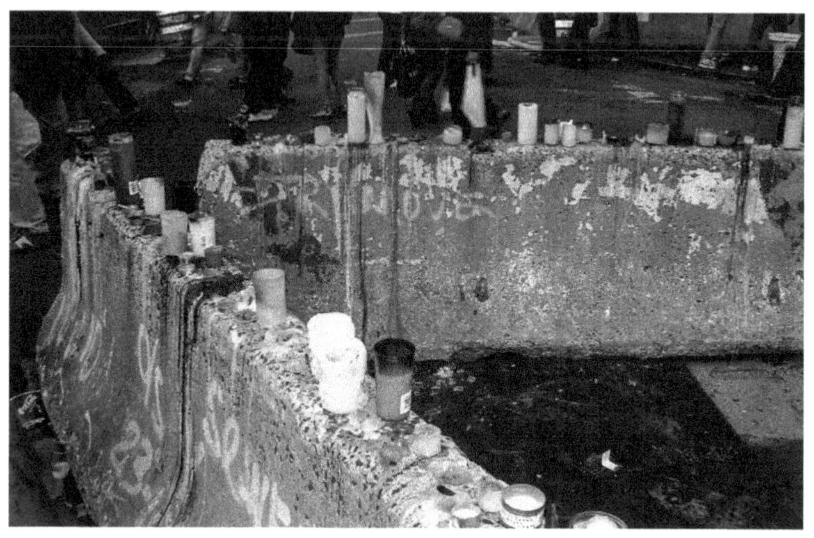

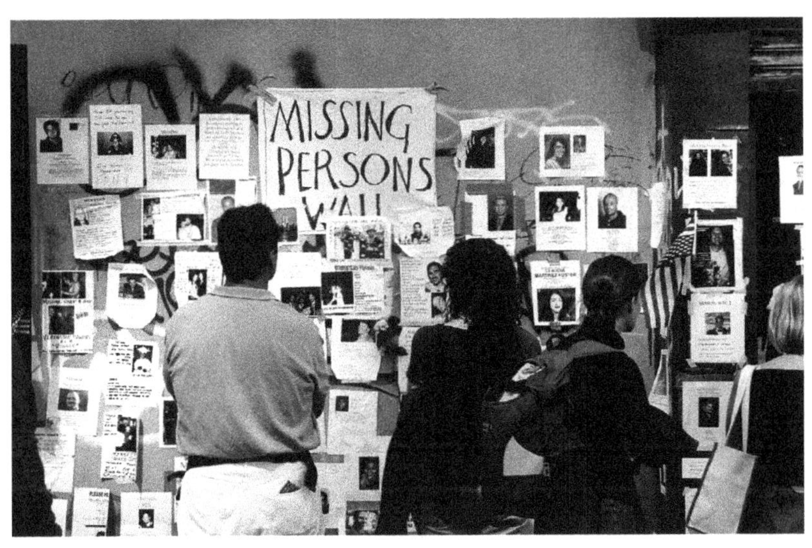

MISSING
PERSONS
WALL

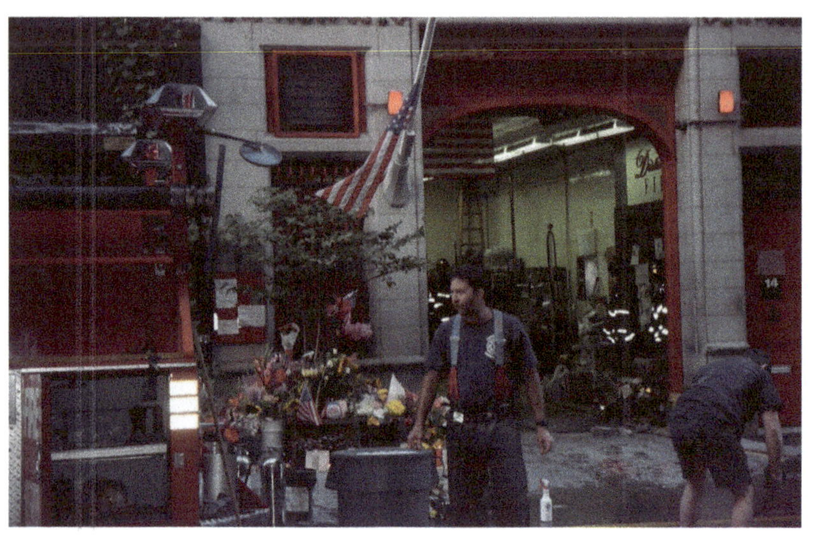

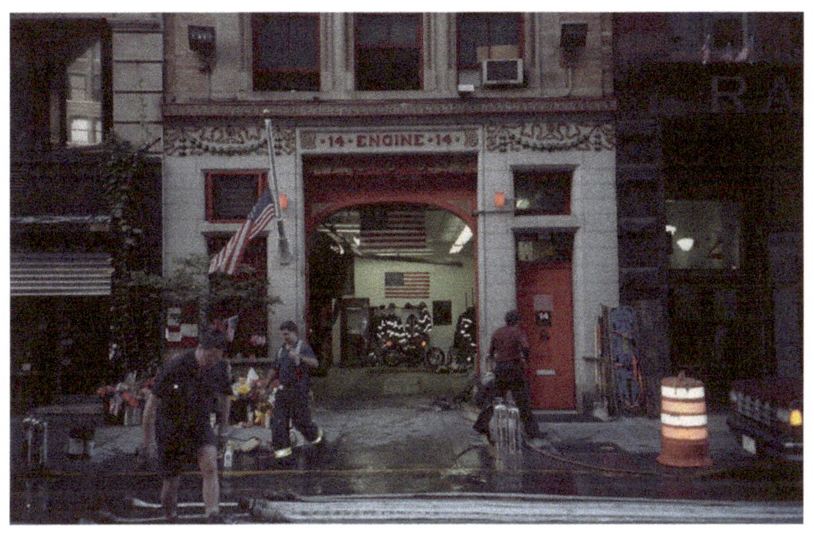

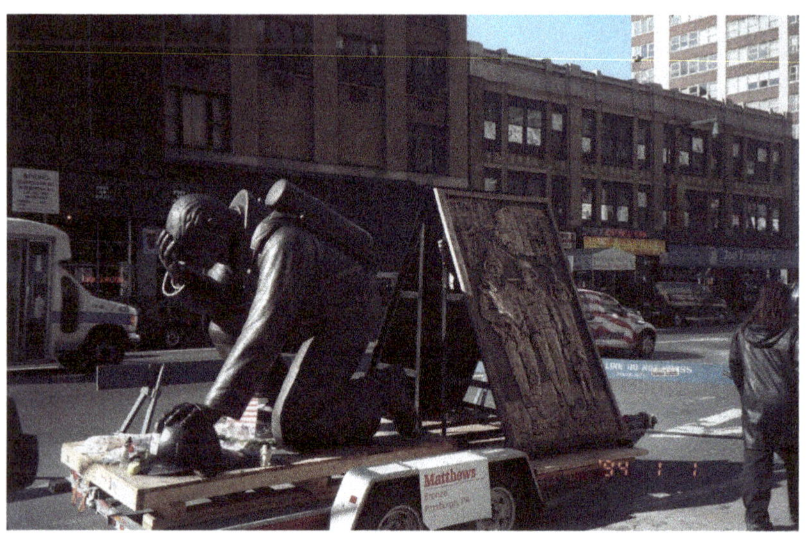

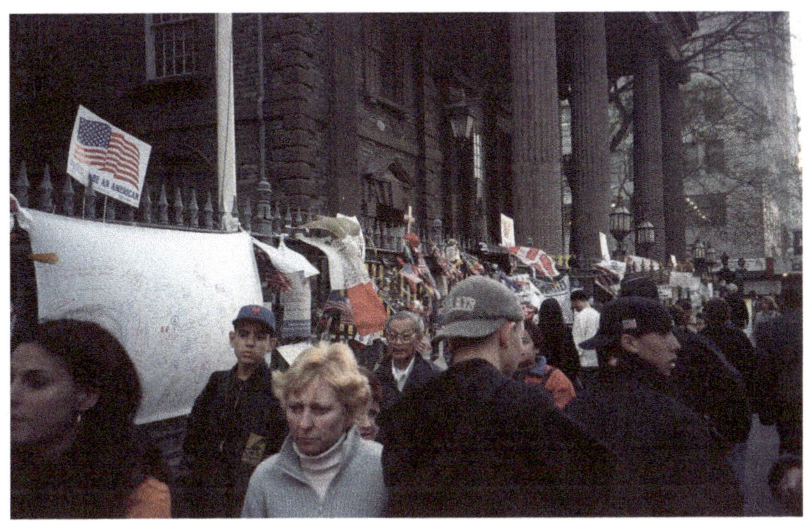

AM AMERICAN

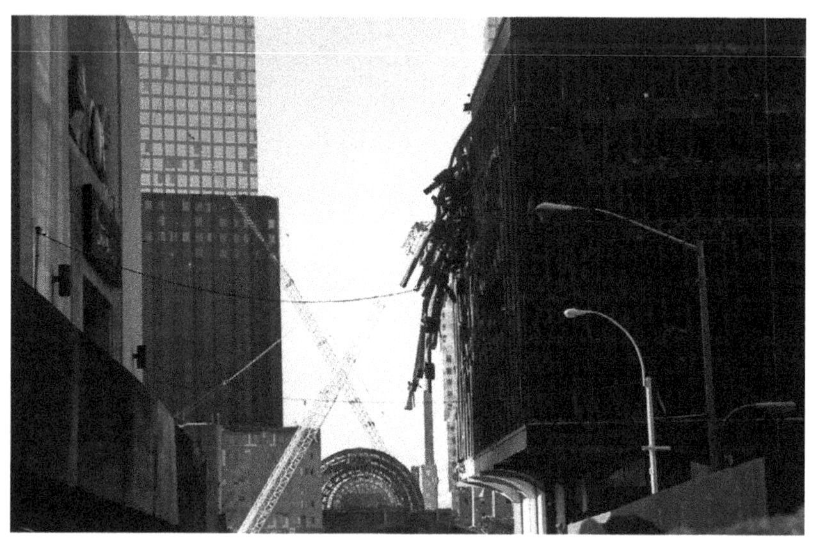

Video Stills

In 2003 I created a video art version of my "from only a mile away" poem. It was premiered at a screening event at St. John's in the Village on 18 August 2004.

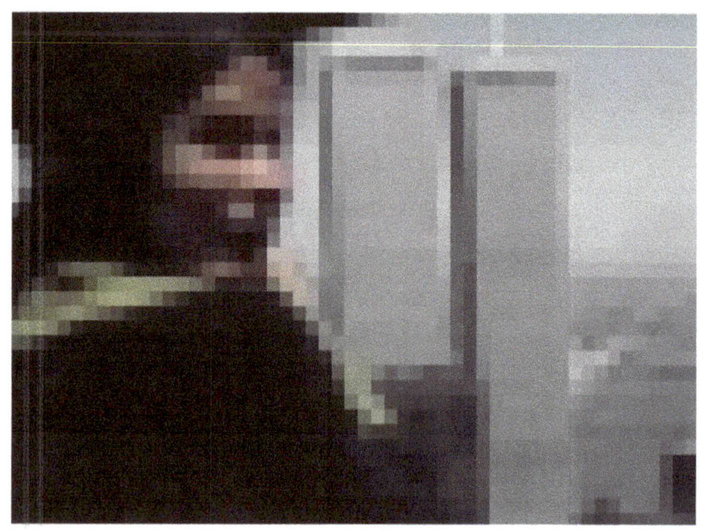

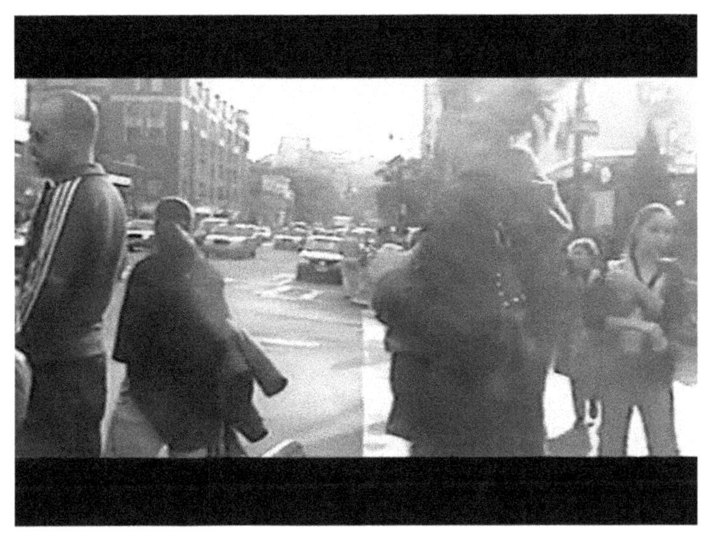

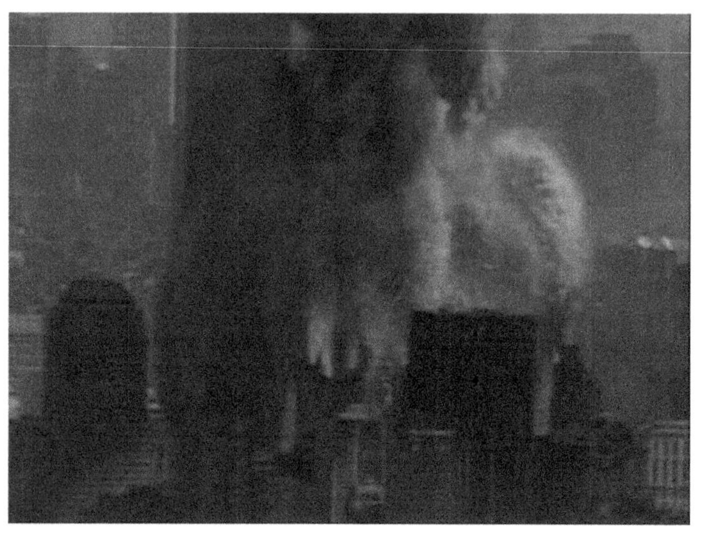

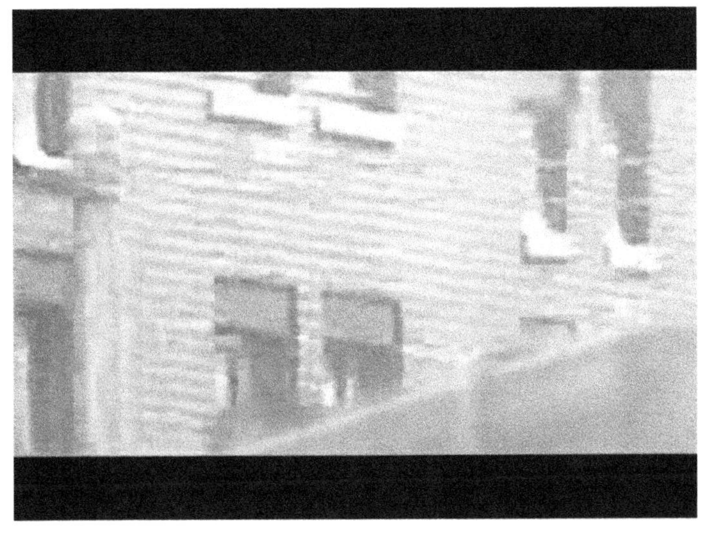

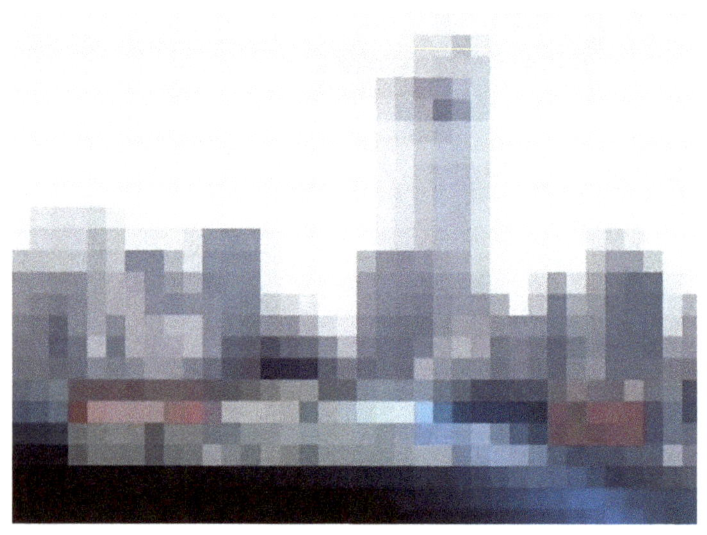

The Language of History

I have published several articles (and the book *Jordan's Journey*) under my family name, Jordan M. Scoggins. These works relate to my family genealogy and the local history of the rural area of Georgia where I am originally from. In "The Language of History," I explored the role of language in defining history and how our choice of words colors our perceptions of that history over time. I used my personal experience witnessing the 9/11 attacks and living through the aftermath as a New Yorker as a backdrop for exploring how quieter, more distant historical memories are depicted, remembered, obscured, glorified, vilified, and forgotten. For me, this article illustrates how history—from the grand narratives we all know and share to the more personal and local stories— is a much more fluid discipline than we often blindly assume.

As a New Yorker, I can't help but wonder how the next generation will look back and remember 9/11. It hardly seems possible that those born just after that terrible day are entering their teen years. That unforgettable day may now seem like ancient history. But I lived it. I watched the Trade Center towers fall with my own eyes. I photographed the buildings as they burned and collapsed. Afterwards, I lived in the no-entry zone and had to show photo ID just to go into my neighborhood. And I stood beside the West Side Highway cheering on the firefighters that sped up and down that thoroughfare for weeks on end.

Sometimes I wonder how my personal experience will fit into the historical narrative of 9/11. Perhaps it won't. History books record grand details and generic overviews of dramatic events, with little space left to present the quiet recollections of those who endured or lived through epic times.

That's the way I grew up and learned history in school in northwest Georgia back in the 1990s. Our textbooks included general descriptions of the Civil War, Reconstruction, the Great Depression, World War II, and other epic chapters in the record of our state, our South, our nation. But it wasn't until I dipped my toe into my family's history that the antiseptic details came alive and became more personal—more real.

Oftentimes when people look at events—events that one day will be studied in history books everywhere—we talk about how much times have changed. In the case of 9/11, we use terms like "terrorism" to try and explain what happened. Language, though, is limiting. The very moment we put words to tongue and pen to paper we somehow fall short. Yet words are something we can't do without. So it's important to be aware of the limitations we create through language, how our own words are confining and how—hopefully—we can transcend them.

When we hear about a violent event—say, when another shooting makes the news—many of us react with a "What's happening to the world?" mindset. The truth is that nothing is happening... at least nothing particularly unusual. We have a tendency to romanticize the past as though it represented some sort of ideal. Nostalgia is something we all experience and it's another way in which language fails us. Matt Novak, writing about the public's perception of the history of the space program, warns that "romanticization of the past has real-world consequences because it breeds a certain kind of futility, a belief that we're simply not able to accomplish things without every American behind the idea."

For most of us, history is learned in language that glorifies the good parts, polishing them beyond what actually happened, while skimming over the bad parts. But those "bad parts" hold a lot of value and can, potentially, teach us just as much if not more than the good things. History is not good. History is not bad. History just… is (or was).

This idea of language and memory applies just as much to the "good ol' days." While reading through old articles in the Summerville News and Walker County Messenger—newspapers from towns close to the seemingly idyllic valley where I was born and raised—I noted a remarkable number of shootings. I focused on these incidents because they felt almost anachronistic at first reading. Aren't guns a relatively modern day problem far removed in time and space from my peaceful valley? Judging by the news from more than a century ago, no.

Here is a report from Villanow, in northwest Georgia's Walker County, in January 1893:

"Wednesday of last week there was a fight in East Armuchee between Bill Short and Dock Kinsey in which the later was badly hurt. At the time West the father of Bill said some hard things of the Goodson's. Saturday there was a good crowd out at the precinct. Between three and four P.M. Jacob Goodson was standing near Cavenders store. Wesley Short called him to one side, as to what followed, there are two statements, one is that Mr. Short was not shot until he had turned to leave. The other is that the conversation ended by Short drawing his knife, raising it and saying with an oath that he was going to cut Goodson's throat. Goodson was prepared and commenced shooting. He emptied his revolver rapidly, three of the five shots taking effect, one struck the bone back of the right ear and ranged around, two hit the right arm, one near and the other above the elbow, the last entered the arm and ranged along it and penetrated the body just below the shoulder. The shooting led to intense excitement in the large crowd. Bailiff Ware immediately arrested Mr. Goodson and deputized Mr. Marshall to take charge of him. As Mr. Goodson thought the excitement would continue as he remained, he and the deputy walked off. Some of his friends followed him, among them his brother, Jesse. Between Jesse and his brother-in-law Charlie Phillips [Author's Note: Charlie Phillips was actually the brother-in-law of Jesse Goodson's wife, not Jesse] there has been bad feeling. After those following Mr. Goodson had gotten off some distance, Charlie was deputized to arrest Jesse. In an exciting manner, he ran after him, Jesse stopped and as he came up, fired at him twice without effect, one ball passed through his clothes. Mr. Phillips returned to the store. Wesley Short, the wounded man, after keeping his feet about 15 minutes, turned sick and was given a bed in the store. Mr. Cavender then had his hack brought out and making him as comfortable as possible, sent him home. Opinion is divided as to his chances for recovery. Some soldiers think he may pull through, while most say the chances are against him. Bond was promptly given by the two brothers, that of Jacob Goodson being fixed by Squire M.G. Clement at $2000.00 and of Jesse at $500.00."

Jacob and Jesse Goodson were my second-great-grand uncles. M.G. Clement was my third-great-grandfather. In reading what otherwise might be a mildly interesting account of an altercation that took place 120 years ago, knowing that my ancestors were involved brought the events to life for me.

While two men having a shoot-out might not sound that unusual, since duels are certainly something we think about in an historical context, such as the Aaron Burr-Alexander Hamilton duel in 1804, I found it surprising that they happened in Armuchee Valley, a land known more for its farms and churches.

Just two months after the Short-Goodson altercation, there was another shooting twenty miles down the road in Gore, a farming community in Dirttown Valley:

"Thomas Morton, son of G.W. Morton, of near Subligna was shot in the leg last Sunday by a man by the name of Bud Stewart. The wound was slight and no serious results will follow. Some difference between the two men came up while at church. They agreed to go off in the woods and settle it, soon after which a pistol shot was heard with the result as above stated. Young Morton walked home after being wounded when Dr. Ballenger cut out the ball and dressed the wound."

I can't imagine settling a score that way! It must have been a serious misunderstanding, though, since G.W. Morton soon left Dirttown Valley for Pinal County, Arizona.

While sometimes these incidents of violence were in the open between dueling antagonists, other shootings were more in the way of ambush. In December 1892, just months before the two duels just described, Reub Suttle, a resident of Subligna—a community halfway between Villanow and Dirttown—was murdered and robbed. The Walker County Messenger reported:

"Thursday [Reub Suttle] was returning with his team, from Rome where he had been to sell a couple of bales of cotton. He stopped at his brother-in-law's George Liles and got supper. He started from there so as to reach home by late bed time. Just before reaching it, the road led through a large enclosure, closed at each end by a gate. When he got to the last gate he was about 200 yards from his home about 10 P.M. When he opened it and led his team through there, death was in store for him. An assassin lay in wait; a shot rang out in the night. As a ball struck him, Reub cried out. His family heard his cries and started to him. Three or four more shots followed in quick succession. The frightened team ran off. When help got there Reub had staggered across the road and was lying dead against a garden fence. Four or five pistol balls had struck him, one in the left side, one about the pit of his stomach and one on the forehead and one in the face. The murderer had done thorough work. One of the shots had been fired at such close range that Reub's shirt had been set on fire. His pockets had been turned inside out. The murderer and his companion, if he had one, had disappeared."

My mother, who would grow up in the area where all this violence took place, though half a century later, sometimes laments how her family used to keep the doors unlocked at night. But judging by Reub Suttle's slaying in 1892, I wonder just how much our nostalgia for the "good old days" misleads us into thinking things were more ideal than they actually were.

When I was a youngster, I recall hearing occasional news stories about a child getting hold of a parent's loaded gun and accidentally pulling the trigger. But according to the old timers, the youth of today are sadly less disciplined and orderly, right? Well, perhaps not:

"The saddest accident that ever occurred in this valley occurred at the residence of Mr. Holcomb's Friday night when Dayton Pledger accidentally shot and killed his brother Bennie. The remains were entered (sic) at Pleasant Grove Sunday. Rev.'s W.C. Cordle and B.F. Hunt conducted the funeral service."

This took place in February 1903 at the home of my second-great-grandfather, William Jackson Holcomb. At the time, Dayton was 13 years old and Bennie was 11.

Two years later, another grim accident occurred when 13-year-old Hill Davis "was shot and instantly killed by his brother [Carl]." The Summerville News reported that the brothers "were out in the field … when a rabbit jumped up in front of them. Carl raised his gun to shoot and just as he pulled the trigger, Hill ran in front of the gun. The whole load hit him in the back of the head, blowing a hole clean through his head and scattering his brains in every direction. Death was instantaneous, the whole top of his head being almost blown off."

It seems that violence—planned or accidental—has always been a part of life. Sometimes it comes in the form of mishaps like the death of little Bennie Pledger. Other times it's on a monumental scale like 9/11. Whether we talk about tragedy or triumph, history's narratives are often just approximations that can be hit and miss. Nobody would remember Bennie Pledger's fate today, for instance, but for that brief snippet in the Summerville News.

In contrast, 9/11 looms large in our consciousness because of the sheer magnitude of the event. But even so, language plays a part in how we remember that day, from the endless media coverage to the repetition of names sculpted into the fountain at the 9/11 Memorial in Manhattan. And yet countless personal stories of those who were there have already been lost to history, because by chance they weren't recorded for newspaper, book, radio, or blog.

The truth is that most of us will never be remembered without words. How many times have you looked at a fading photo and wished someone had written down a name to identify the person, place and time? Language is what allows us to preserve the memories of those who came before us. Language helps us grasp the undefinable. And, even when we get it wrong, the effort is not futile, because it sparks our imagination and can bring to life even the driest historical accounts.

About the Artist

luke kurtis (also known as Jordan M. Scoggins) is a Georgia-born interdisciplinary artist focusing on the intersection of photography, writing, and design. He has exhibited work in galleries and alternative spaces around the country. His debut solo museum exhibition, *INTERSECTION*, featured photography and writing and opened at Massillon Museum in March 2014. His multimedia project *Jordan's Journey* used genealogical and historical research as a device to explore the idea of personal and collective memory. Related articles and photography have appeared in *Georgia Backroads*. Other publications include the *INTERSECTION* zine featuring his original writing and art as well as his poetry collections *let us prey* (featured in RikArt Artist Book Collection, Rikhardinkatu Library, Helsinki, Finland) and *quilt*. His work has also appeared in *The Emerson Review*, *Encounters*, *Iceland Review*, *The Red Truck Review*, *Skin To Skin*, and *S/tick: Feminists on Guard*. In 2012 he co-founded New Lit Salon Press. He lives and works in New York City's Greenwich Village. Visit luke at http://lukekurtis.com